Celebrated Lyrical Solos

BOOK 2

9 Solos in Romantic Styles for Early Intermediate Pianists

Robert D. Vandall

W0007085

Students all love to play fast and showy pieces, but there is another side to performing that needs to be developed: the lyrical side. Beautiful melodies need to be shaped musically and balanced properly against the accompaniment. The ability to bend the tempo and play with flexibility also results in expressive playing. Colorful harmonies and their movement can create a sound world that can be molded into beautiful moments as well.

The pieces in *Celebrated Lyrical Solos, Book 2* are designed to aid students with musicality when playing lyrical music. I have endeavored to include pieces with a variety of tempos and moods. While every piece may not necessarily focus on lyrical styles throughout, each has a section that will help students develop skills in lyrical playing. Look for the many ways that the pieces in these books can be balanced and molded into something beautiful. Feel, listen and enjoy the many lyrical moods of these solos.

Robert D. Vandall

Contents

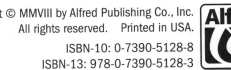

Lucky Day

Robert D. Vandall

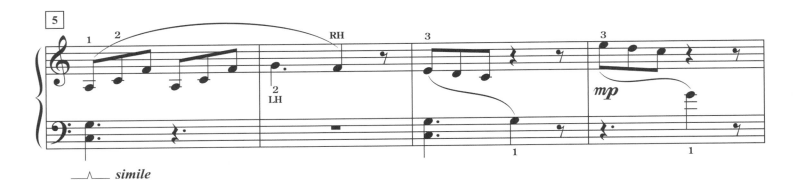

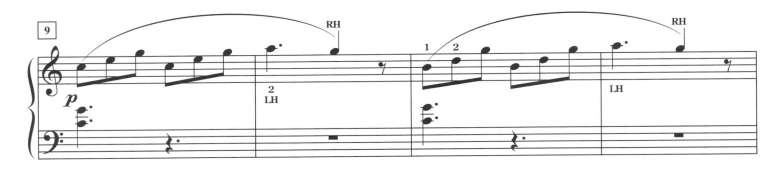

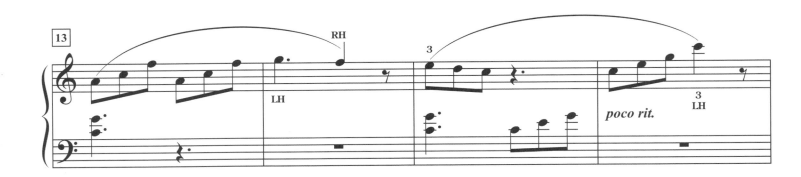

3

4

Carillon Dance

Robert D. Vandall

Footprints

Robert D. Vandall

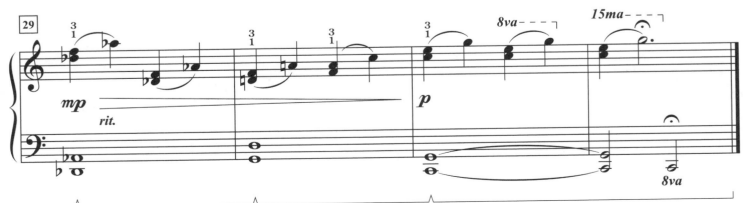

Winter Night

Robert D. Vandall

11

Whirlpools

Robert D. Vandall

One More Dance

Robert D. Vandall

Greenbrier

Robert D. Vandall

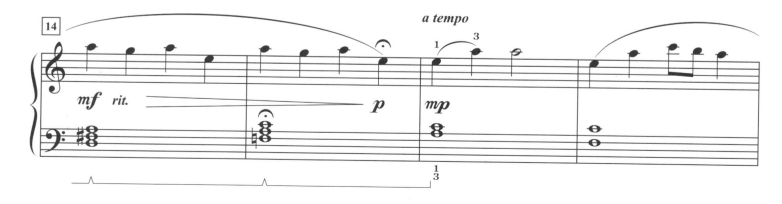

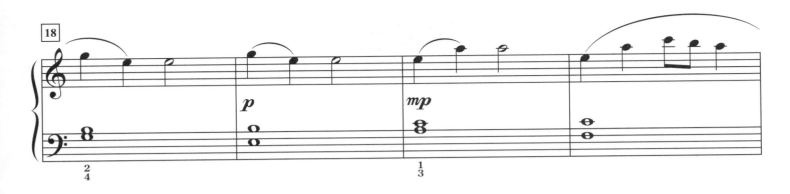

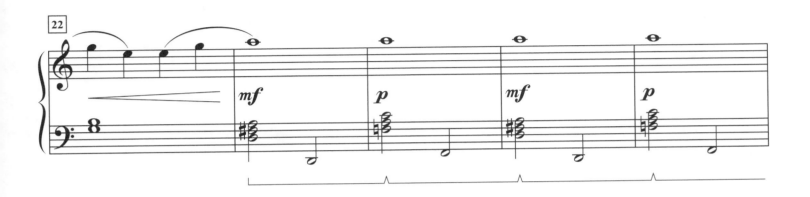

Meno mosso

Cascades

Robert D. Vandall

Summer Dream

Robert D. Vandall

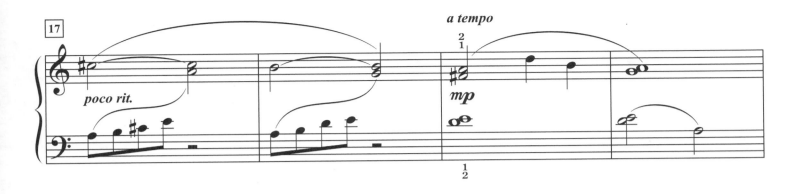

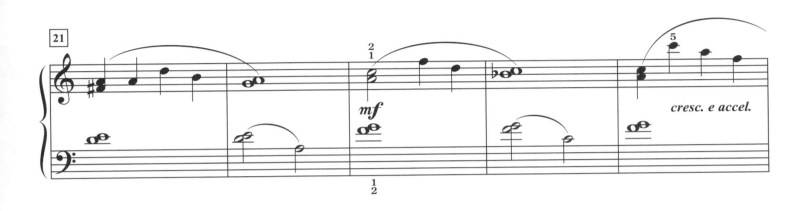

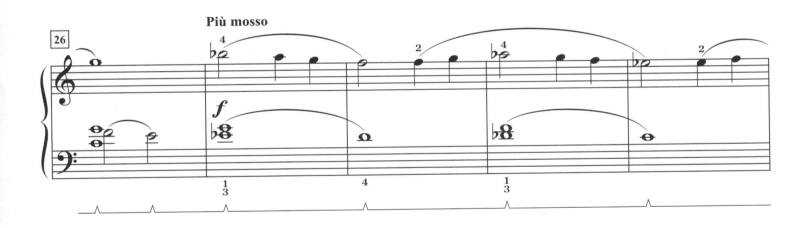

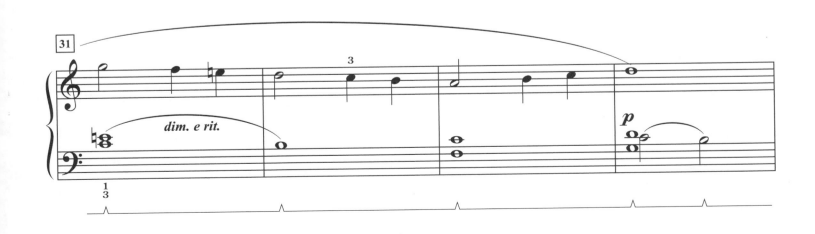